AICPA® & CIMA®

Worldwide leaders in public and management accounting

AF788626

Audit Risk Alert

2018/19 | *Government Auditing Standards* and Single Audit Developments

Strengthening Audit Integrity
Safeguarding Financial Reporting

AICPA®

A resource of the
Enhancing Audit
Quality Initiative

23574-349

1 2 3 4 5 6 7 8 9 0 AAP 1 9 8

ISBN 978-1-94830-627-0 (print)

ISBN 978-1-94830-628-7 (ePub)

Notice to Readers

This Audit Risk Alert (alert) replaces Government Auditing Standards *and Single Audit Developments — 2017/2018*.

This alert provides auditors who perform audits under *Government Auditing Standards* and Title 2 *U.S. Code of Federal Regulations* Part 200, *Uniform Administrative Requirements, Cost Principles, and Audit Requirements for Federal Awards* (Uniform Guidance), with an overview of recent industry, technical, regulatory, and professional developments that may affect the audits and other engagements they perform. As well, an entity's internal management can use this alert to address areas of audit concern.

This publication is an *other auditing publication,* as defined in AU-C section 200, *Overall Objectives of the Independent Auditor and the Conduct of an Audit in Accordance With Generally Accepted Auditing Standards*.[1] Other auditing publications have no authoritative status; however, they may help the auditor understand and apply generally accepted auditing standards.

In applying the auditing guidance included in an other auditing publication, the auditor should, using professional judgment, assess the relevance and appropriateness of such guidance to the circumstances of the audit. The auditing guidance in this document has been reviewed by the AICPA Audit and Attest Standards staff and published by the AICPA and is presumed to be appropriate. This document has not been approved, disapproved, or otherwise acted on by a senior technical committee of the AICPA.

Recognition

Reviewers

Governmental Audit Quality Center Executive Committee Members

Erica Forhan, *Chairperson*
Ron Conrad
Michael Fritz
John Good
Brittney Williams
Jeff Winter

Other Reviewers

Ralph DeAcetis
Terry Ramsey
George Rippey

AICPA Staff

Susan M. Reed
Manager
Product Management & Development — Public Accounting

Teresa Bordeaux
Lead Manager
Governmental Auditing and Accounting

The AICPA gratefully acknowledges those members of the Auditing Standards Board and Governmental Audit Quality Center Executive Committee who helped identify the interest areas for inclusion in this alert.

---

[1] All AU-C sections can be found in AICPA *Professional Standards*.

Feedback

Audit Risk Alert Government Auditing Standards *and Single Audit Developments* is published annually. As you encounter audit or industry issues that you believe warrant discussion in next year's alert, please feel free to share them with us. Any other comments you have about the alert also would be appreciated. You may email these comments to a&apublications@aicpa-cima.com.

TABLE OF CONTENTS

How This Alert Helps You

.01 This Audit Risk Alert (alert) helps you plan and perform audits conducted in accordance with generally accepted government auditing standards (GAGAS) as set forth in *Government Auditing Standards* (also known as the Yellow Book) and Title 2 U.S. *Code of Federal Regulations* Part 200, *Uniform Administrative Requirements, Cost Principles, and Audit Requirements for Federal Awards* (Uniform Guidance). Additionally, an entity's internal management can use this alert to address areas of audit concern. This alert provides information to assist you in achieving a more robust understanding of the requirements for performing a single audit, including issues that may be encountered as part of performing the compliance audit under the Uniform Guidance. This alert is an important tool to help you identify the significant risks that may affect the audit, and it delivers information about emerging practice issues and current auditing and regulatory developments as they relate to audits performed under *Government Auditing Standards* and Uniform Guidance requirements. For developing issues that may have a significant impact on single audits in the future, the "On the Horizon" section provides information on these topics.

.02 Single audits are a complex and evolving practice area. It is an area that requires you, the auditor, to keep up to date throughout the year with developments that affect the single audits performed. This includes not only the audit requirements related to single audits, but also agency policies and requirements related to federal awards and other related developments. This alert is a good resource for the following:

- To help you assess whether you are appropriately applying *Government Auditing Standards* and the Uniform Guidance requirements in your single audits
- To assist you in proper implementation of the guidance
- To assist you in keeping up with developments related to single audits

.03 Use this alert in conjunction with Audit Risk Alert *General Accounting and Auditing Developments — 2018/19*, which explains important issues that affect all entities in all industries in the current economic climate. In addition, you may want to use this alert in conjunction with Audit Risk Alert *Not-for-Profit Entities Industry Developments — 2018*. You should refer to the full text of accounting and auditing pronouncements as well as the full text of any rules or publications that this alert discusses.

.04 In an audit performed under generally accepted auditing standards (GAAS) and *Government Auditing Standards*, it is essential that you understand the meaning of audit risk and the interaction of audit risk with the objective of obtaining sufficient appropriate audit evidence. Auditors obtain audit evidence to draw reasonable conclusions on which to base their opinion on compliance by performing the following:

- Risk assessment procedures
- Further audit procedures that comprise
    - tests of controls, when required by GAAS, *Government Auditing Standards*, regulation (such as the Uniform Guidance), or when the auditor has chosen to do so; and

— substantive audit procedures performed to gather evidence related to the opinion on compliance that include tests of details and analytical procedures

.05 You should develop an audit plan that includes, among other things, the nature and extent of planned risk assessment procedures as determined under AU-C section 315, *Understanding the Entity and Its Environment and Assessing the Risks of Material Misstatement.*[2] AU-C section 315 defines *risk assessment procedures* as "the audit procedures performed to obtain an understanding of the entity and its environment, including the entity's internal control, to identify and assess the risks of material misstatement, whether due to fraud or error, at the financial statement and relevant assertion levels." As part of obtaining the required understanding of the entity and its environment, paragraph .12 of AU-C section 315 states that the auditor should obtain an understanding of the industry, regulatory, and other external factors, including the applicable financial reporting framework, relevant to the entity. This alert assists the auditor with this aspect of the risk assessment procedures and further expands the auditor's understanding of other important considerations relevant to the audit.

.06 In an audit performed under GAAS and *Government Auditing Standards*, risk assessment procedures should be performed for all aspects of the audit. They are performed as part of the audit of the financial statements and to address the additional reporting required under *Government Auditing Standards*. Furthermore, AU-C section 935, *Compliance Audits*, provides guidance and requirements regarding risk assessment in compliance audits. In applying AU-C section 935 to a Uniform Guidance compliance audit, the auditor should perform risk assessment procedures for each of the major programs to obtain a sufficient understanding of the direct and material compliance requirements and the entity's internal control over compliance with those direct and material compliance requirements. This understanding establishes a frame of reference within which the auditor plans the compliance audit and exercises professional judgment about assessing risks of material noncompliance and responding to those risks throughout the compliance audit.

.07 This alert does not include all information that may be important or relevant to a single audit and is not intended to be a complete listing of auditor considerations regarding the requirements when planning and performing a compliance audit under the Uniform Guidance. Instead, this alert highlights some key points or areas of significant change for the auditor to consider.

Revision to *Government Auditing Standards*

Introduction

.08 The Government Accountability Office (GAO) issued *Government Auditing Standards, 2018 Revision* on July 17, 2018. It is effective for financial audits, attestation engagements, and reviews of financial statements for fiscal periods ending on or after June 30, 2020. It is effective for performance audits beginning on or after July 1, 2019. Early implementation is not permitted. Although the 2018 Yellow Book is not effective for single audits until June 30, 2020 fiscal year-ends and later, auditors need to keep in mind that the 2018

[2] All AU-C sections can be found in AICPA *Professional Standards*.

Yellow Book has revised the independence standards. Because auditors need to be independent for the entire period under audit, consideration of the independence requirements of the 2018 Yellow Book is needed prior to the effective date. For example, an auditor performing a June 30, 2020, single audit will need to comply with the new independence requirements at the beginning of the audit period — that is, July 1, 2019.

.09 This section of the alert highlights requirements and guidance found in the 2018 Yellow Book. It primarily presents areas of the standards that have changed. In some cases, the topic is simply a mention; in others, more detail is provided. It is important that auditors read and understand the standards in full in order to prepare for its effective date.

Format and Organization

.10 One significant change found in the 2018 Yellow Book is that the overall format of the guidance has been revised to separate the requirements under *Government Auditing Standards* from any application guidance. Each requirement (or set of requirements) is located in a box with the application guidance shown in subsequent paragraphs. This change in format more clearly distinguishes between the actual requirement and the information included in the standards to assist in the requirement's application.

.11 In addition, chapter content has been reorganized both within chapters and between chapters. The 2011 Yellow Book contains seven chapters; the 2018 Yellow Book contains nine chapters. One example of the reorganization is that the topics found in chapter 3, "General Standards," of the 2011 Yellow Book are located in three different chapters in the 2018 Yellow Book. Note that the topics of independence, professional judgment, competence, and quality control and assurance are no longer referred to as "general standards."

Independence

.12 Independence is one area of significant change in the 2018 Yellow Book, especially as it relates to nonaudit service independence requirements. Due to the format changes that separate the requirements from the application guidance, the Yellow Book requirements related to independence are much clearer. Furthermore, the independence standards and application guidance has been expanded as it relates to nonaudit services. Some items of note include the following:

- The requirement found at paragraph 3.88 in the independence standard states that auditors should conclude that preparing financial statements in their entirety from a client-provided trial balance or underlying accounting records creates significant threats, and auditors should document the threats and safeguards applied to eliminate and reduce threats to an acceptable level or decline to perform the service.
- The revised independence standards require the auditor to evaluate and document that evaluation of the significance of threats related to any nonprohibited nonaudit services associated with any preparation of accounting records and financial statements.
- As part of evaluating threats to independence, the auditor considers management's ability to effectively oversee the nonaudit service to be provided. Application guidance is provided at paragraph

3.79 regarding indicators of management's ability to effectively oversee the nonaudit services. These include considering management's ability to determine the reasonableness of the results of the nonaudit services provided and to recognize a material error, omission, or misstatement in the results of the nonaudit services provided.

.13 Furthermore, the documentation requirements related to independence have been modified. Paragraph 3.107 sets forth the requirements for documenting the threats to independence and safeguards applied, the auditor's understanding with an audited entity for which the auditor will provide a nonaudit service (which includes the audited entity's acceptance of its responsibilities), and the consideration of management's ability to effectively oversee a nonaudit service to be provided by the auditor, all of which are found in the 2011 Yellow Book. However, also included in the 2018 Yellow Book documentation requirements is an explicit requirement to document the evaluation of the significance of the threats created by providing any of the services discussed in paragraph 3.89. The services listed in that paragraph include the following:

- Recording transactions for which management has determined or approved the appropriate account classification, or posting coded transactions to an audited entity's general ledger
- Preparing certain line items or sections of the financial statements based on information in the trial balance
- Posting entries that an audited entity's management has approved to the entity's trial balance
- Preparing account reconciliations that identify reconciling items for the audited entity management's evaluation

.14 The 2018 Yellow Book includes two flowcharts at the end of chapter 3 that further illustrate the independence requirements. Figure 1, "Generally Accepted Government Auditing Standards Conceptual Framework for Independence," covers threats to independence in general. Figure 1 refers the user to figure 2, "Independence Considerations for Preparing Accounting Records and Financial Statements," when the consideration is regarding those specific nonaudit services.

.15 Overall, the consideration of nonaudit services by the auditor is given increased emphasis under the 2018 Yellow Book. This is an area that needs to be considered early on because an auditor is required to be independent from an audited entity during any period of time that falls within the period covered by the financial statements or subject matter of the engagement and the period of the professional engagement. For a June 30, 2020 year-end single audit, the first fiscal year-end for which the 2018 Yellow Book is effective, the auditor is required to be in compliance with the independence standards of the 2018 Yellow Book at July 1, 2019.

Competence

.16 The competence standard under the 2018 Yellow Book retains the requirements found in the 2011 Yellow Book. However, application guidance has been added that clarifies what may be indicators of competence and what competence for an assigned role means. Further guidance is provided regarding the levels of *Government Auditing Standards* proficiency expected for different roles on an engagement.

Continuing Professional Education

.17 The requirements for continuing professional education (CPE) in the 2018 Yellow Book retain the same CPE hour requirements as found previously. Application guidance has been added on a number of topics related to obtaining CPE, and is generally based on the guidance found in the document, "Government Auditing Standards: Guidance on GAGAS Requirements for Continuing Professional Education (April 2005)," which will be superseded upon the effective date of the 2018 Yellow Book. Included in the application guidance is information regarding what qualifies as Yellow Book CPE, including what subject matter may qualify for each of the following categories:

- Subject matter directly related to the government environment, government auditing, or the specific or unique environment in which the audited entity operates (24-hour requirement)
- Subject matter that directly enhances auditors' professional expertise to conduct engagements (56-hour requirement)

.18 Application guidance has also been added that emphasizes the need to obtain GAGAS-specific CPE, particularly in years in which there have been revisions to the standards, as that may assist auditors in maintaining the competence necessary to conduct GAGAS engagements. Also added is an exception to the CPE requirements found in paragraph 4.16 of the 2018 Yellow Book for nonsupervisory staff who charge less than 40 hours of their time annually to engagements conducted under GAGAS.

.19 It is suggested that auditors review their CPE policies and procedures to ensure they are consistent with the 2018 Yellow Book before it becomes effective.

Quality Control

.20 The 2018 Yellow Book content related to quality control is expanded. The quality control standard clarifies that the audit organization is required to establish policies and procedures designed to provide reasonable assurance that the audit organization only undertakes engagements it has the capability to perform, including a consideration of both time and resources. Other requirements are added, and guidance provided, for engagement performance, documentation, and reporting policies and procedures pertaining to the review and supervision of engagement work performed by the engagement team. Furthermore, the guidance regarding monitoring of quality are expanded to describe the information that should be included in the monitoring and provides requirements regarding an evaluation of the monitoring.

.21 One explicit requirement is that an audit organization is required to obtain, at least annually, written affirmation of compliance with policies and procedures on independence from those personnel required to be independent.

Peer Review

.22 The content regarding peer review in the 2018 Yellow Book has been modified to differentiate the requirements for those audit organizations affiliated with a recognized organization. Audit organizations affiliated with any one of five recognized organizations are required to comply with the respective organization's peer review requirements and several additional requirements described throughout paragraphs 5.66.80 of the 2018 Yellow Book. The recognized organizations include the following:

- American Institute of Certified Public Accountants
- Council of the Inspectors General on Integrity and Efficiency
- Association of Local Government Auditors
- International Organization of Supreme Audit Institutions
- National State Auditors Association

.23 Any audit organization not affiliated with one of the recognized organizations is subject to a longer list of GAGAS peer review requirements as described throughout paragraphs 5.66.94.

.24 A flowchart in figure 3, "Developing Peer Review Communications for Observed Matters in Accordance with Generally Accepted Government Auditing Standards," provides additional assistance for peer reviewers in terms of applying the requirements in paragraphs 5.725.74 regarding the evaluation of observed matters and the related documentation and communication of that evaluation.

Standards for Financial Audits

Waste

.25 The 2011 Yellow Book includes auditor requirements related to abuse when an auditor becomes aware of abuse. The 2018 Yellow Book transitions the discussion of abuse to application guidance and adds the concept of waste, which is not found in the Uniform Guidance. Waste is defined as the act of using or expending resources carelessly, extravagantly, or to no purpose. Waste can include activities that do not include abuse and does not necessarily involve a violation of law. Waste relates primarily to mismanagement, inappropriate actions, and inadequate oversight.

.26 The 2018 Yellow Book states that evaluating internal control in a government environment may also include considering internal control deficiencies that result in waste or abuse. However, under that guidance, auditors are not required to perform specific procedures to detect waste or abuse in financial audits. Auditors may consider whether and how to communicate such matters if they become aware of them. Auditors may also discover that waste or abuse is indicative of fraud or noncompliance with provisions of laws, regulations, contracts, and grant agreements. Examples of waste and abuse are also provided.

Note: The change in the 2018 Yellow Book regarding abuse introduces a difference between the Uniform Guidance and the Yellow Book on the treatment of abuse. The Uniform Guidance still requires an auditor to report abuse found based on the guidance in 2 CFR 200.516, which states that the auditor must report significant deficiencies and material weaknesses in internal control over major programs and significant instances of abuse relating to major programs. The auditor's determination of whether a deficiency in internal control is a significant deficiency or material weakness for the purpose of reporting an audit finding is in relation to a type of compliance requirement for a major program identified in the Compliance Supplement. Findings

Findings

.27 The 2018 Yellow Book clarifies that the auditor is required to consider internal control deficiencies in the auditor's evaluation of identified findings when developing the cause element of a finding. Application guidance notes that, regardless of the type of finding identified, the cause of a finding may relate to one or more underlying internal control deficiencies. Depending on magnitude of impact, likelihood of occurrence, and the nature of the deficiency, the deficiency could be a significant deficiency or material weakness in a financial audit.

Licensing and Certification

.28 A requirement is added related to auditors working outside the U.S. In that case, auditors who do not work for a government audit organization should meet the qualifications noted in paragraph 6.04 of the 2018 Yellow Book, have certifications that meet all applicable national and international standards and serve in their respective countries as the functional equivalent of CPAs in the U.S., or work for nongovernmental audit organizations that are the functional equivalent of licensed certified public accounting firms in the U.S.

Attestation Engagements and Reviews of Financial Statements

.29 The 2018 Yellow Book adds standards for review engagements. Furthermore, the chapter related to attestation and review engagements has been updated to reflect the issuance of Statement on Standards for Attestation Engagements (SSAE) No. 18, *Attestation Standards: Clarification and Recodification,*[3] and Statement on Standards for Accounting and Review Services (SSARS) No. 21, *Statements on Standards for Accounting and Review Services: Clarification and Recodification.*[4] In addition, the concept of waste was added to the guidance related to an examination type of attestation engagement that is consistent with that found in the standards for financial audits.

Performance Audits

.30 Revisions have been made to the guidance related to performance audits, including the clarification that management assertions are not required when conducting a performance audit. The performance audit standards are also updated with specific considerations for when internal control is significant to the audit objectives. In addition, the concept of waste is added consistent with that found in the standards for financial audits.

Other Revisions

.31 There were several other changes of note in the 2018 Yellow Book as follows:

- It expands its discussion of the engagement teams' evaluation of the qualifications and competency of specialists.
- Application guidance is added in the reporting area covering situations such as the effect on the Yellow Book report when there is

---

[3] Statement on Standards for Attestation Engagements No. 18, *Attestation Standards: Clarification and Recodification,* is codified in the AT-C sections in AICPA *Professional Standards*.

[4] Statement on Standards for Accounting and Review Services No. 21, *Statements on Standards for Accounting and Review Services: Clarification and Recodification,* is codified in the AR-C sections in AICPA *Professional Standards*.

a disclaimer of opinion, or when comparative financial statements are presented.

- Supplemental guidance from the 2011 revision of the Yellow Book is either removed or incorporated into the individual chapters.
- The documents titled Government Auditing Standards: *Guidance on GAGAS Requirements for Continuing Professional Education* (GAO-05-568G, April 2005) and Government Auditing Standards: *Guidance for Understanding the New Peer Review Ratings* (D06602, January 2014) are being retired upon the effective date of the 2018 Yellow Book. Relevant guidance and information from these documents have been incorporated directly into the 2018 Yellow Book, as appropriate.
- Minor wording changes were made throughout the standards.
- A glossary of terms was added.

Office of Management and Budget

OMB *Compliance Supplement*

.32 Each year, the Office of Management and Budget (OMB) issues a *Compliance Supplement* to be used by auditors in performing a single audit. The Uniform Guidance references the annual *Compliance Supplement* as the source of compliance requirements that the federal government expects to be considered as part of a single audit. Therefore, the *Compliance Supplement* is one of the most important pieces of guidance an auditor uses in performing single audits.

.33 The 2018 *Compliance Supplement* is effective for single audits of fiscal years beginning after June 30, 2017, (that is, years ending June 30, 2018, and later). In past years, the *Compliance Supplement* for the year issued superseded the prior year's supplement in its entirety. However, that is not the case for the 2018 *Compliance Supplement.* This is because the 2018 *Compliance Supplement* was issued in a different format than in prior years and provides only significant updates and changes to the 2017 *Compliance Supplement.* Therefore, auditors must use both the 2017 and 2018 supplements when performing audits of fiscal years for which the 2018 *Compliance Supplement* is effective; that is, fiscal years ending on or after June 30, 2018. The most current and previous year's editions can be found at https://www.whitehouse.gov/omb/management/office-federal-financial-management/.

.34 The 2018 *Compliance Supplement* adds, deletes, and modifies prior supplement sections as usual. However, unlike prior years' supplements, the 2018 *Compliance Supplement* modifies only sections of the 2017 *Compliance Supplement* that were in need of significant revisions. Any sections from the 2017 *Compliance Supplement* that did not have revisions made to them were not copied into the 2018 *Compliance Supplement.* As a result, for audits requiring the use of the 2018 *Compliance Supplement,* auditors must refer to the 2017 *Compliance Supplement* for information that was not carried over to the 2018 *Compliance Supplement.*

.35 While auditors may not be used to focusing in on part 1 and the table of contents, it will be very important to do so when using the 2018

Compliance Supplement because they provide information about how to use the supplement. The table of contents in the 2018 *Compliance Supplement* describes where it adds, deletes, or supersedes sections in the 2017 *Compliance Supplement*. It provides important information regarding which supplement (2017 or 2018) to use for a particular part (or section of that part) of the supplement. For example, the information in the table of contents indicates that, for some federal agencies, the auditor should use only the relevant section of the 2017 *Compliance Supplement*. For others, the auditor should use only the relevant section of the 2018 *Compliance Supplement*. Finally, for some agencies, the auditor will use the 2017 *Compliance Supplement* for some programs and the 2018 *Compliance Supplement* for others.

.36

2018 *Compliance Supplement* resource available on GAQC website

OMB posted only a single PDF version of the 2018 *Compliance Supplement* on the OMB website. However, as a public service for auditors, the Governmental Audit Quality Center (GAQC) has posted a resource that contains both the 2018 *Compliance Supplement* and the 2017 *Compliance Supplement*, by section, with information about which supplement, or supplements, to use in a given situation. The 2017 *Compliance Supplement* files posted include a watermark that indicates those sections of the 2017 *Compliance Supplement* that were superseded by the 2018 *Compliance Supplement*. The marking of the 2017 *Compliance Supplement* files has been done to help auditors avoid using a superseded or deleted section of the 2017 *Compliance Supplement* and is nonauthoritative. In addition, the resource lists key auditor considerations for particular parts of the supplement. This resource is available to the public and can be found at https://www.aicpa.org/interestareas/governmentalauditquality/resources/singleaudit/2018-omb-compliance-supplement.html.

Uniform Guidance Procurement Requirements

.37 After several grace periods granted by OMB, the Uniform Guidance procurement requirements are now effective for those entities that elected to continue using previous guidance. The three-year grace period extended the effective date for the application of the Uniform Guidance procurement requirements to fiscal years beginning on or after December 26, 2017. Therefore, an entity with a June 30 year-end is required to be in compliance with the Uniform Guidance procurement requirements for the year beginning July 1, 2018. Because most entities did not early adopt the new procurement requirements, many auditors will not be auditing compliance with the Uniform Guidance procurement requirements until their 2019 single audits. Auditors in that situation should be using Part 3.1, section I, "Procurement and Suspension and Debarment," of the 2017 *Compliance Supplement* for compliance testing of procurement. Otherwise, the updated Part 3.2, section I, "Procurement and Suspension and Debarment" in the 2018 *Compliance Supplement* should be used by auditors when testing this requirement for entities that have adopted the Uniform Guidance procurement requirements.

.38 Upon implementing the Uniform Guidance procurement requirements, a nonfederal entity must have written procurement policies and procedures that reflect the applicable requirements of the Uniform Guidance. It is important that a nonfederal entity's written procurement policies and procedures address each requirement (indicated by the use of "must") found in the Uniform Guidance procurement requirements, as applicable.

.39 Procurement is an area in which compliance issues are frequently found. As part of implementing the Uniform Guidance procurement requirements, it is suggested that nonfederal entities place emphasis on training staff regarding the updated procurement policies and procedures. In addition, a system for monitoring procurement procedures is a core element in establishing a strong, effective procurement system. As a best practice, auditors may also wish to consider beginning to train staff on the new procurement requirements in advance of staff having to audit them and in the event auditees have questions during their implementation of the new requirements.

.40 OMB Memorandum M-18-18 The National Defense Authorization Act for Fiscal Year 2017 (2017 NDAA) raised the micro-purchase threshold to $10,000 for procurements under grants and cooperative agreements for institutions of higher education, or related or affiliated not-for-profit entities, not-for-profit research organizations, or independent research institutes (covered entities). It also established a process whereby covered entities can request, and federal agencies can approve, a higher micro-purchase threshold. The National Defense Authorization Act for Fiscal Year 2018 (2018 NDAA) raised the threshold for micro-purchases to $10,000 and the threshold for simplified acquisitions to $250,000 for all recipients. However, for the 2018 NDAA provisions, 2 CFR 200.67 and 2 CFR 200.88 require that any increases in the thresholds are not effective until implemented in the Federal Acquisition Regulations (FAR).

.41 In order to allow maximum flexibility for grant recipients in light of the 2018 NDAA, OMB is granting an exception allowing recipients to use the higher threshold in advance of revisions to the FAR and the Uniform Guidance. OMB memorandum M-18-18, "Implementing Statutory Changes to the Micro-Purchase and Simplified Acquisition Thresholds for Financial Assistance," (the memorandum) was issued on June 20, 2018, to implement the changes to the micro-purchase and simplified acquisition thresholds for financial assistance under the 2017 and 2018 NDAA. Agencies are required to implement these changes in the terms and conditions of their awards, and recipients of existing federal financial assistance may implement the new thresholds in their internal controls. The memorandum also implements an approval process for those institutions that requested a higher micro-purchase threshold. The memorandum clarifies that the increased threshold for covered entities under the 2017 NDAA was effective when the act was signed; that is, December 23, 2016. The effective date of the increased thresholds under the 2018 NDAA, which is applicable to all recipients, is the date of issuance of the memorandum; that is, June 20, 2018.

.42 The procurement requirements and audit advisory made prior to the issuance of M-18-18 are discussed in the 2018 *Compliance Supplement* in Part 3.2, section I, "Procurement and Suspension and Debarment" and Appendix VII-A, section II, "National Defense Authorization Acts (NDAA) of 2017 and 2018." Auditors should refer to this information for guidance when auditing procurement.

Federal Agency and Other Activities

President's Management Agenda

.43 The President's Management Agenda, issued in March 2018, provides a long-term vision for modernizing the federal government in key areas that will improve the ability of all agencies to deliver mission outcomes, provide excellent service, and effectively steward taxpayer dollars on behalf of the American people. The Management Agenda includes a number of cross-agency priority goals to address government-wide challenges that cut across federal agencies, along with strategies for achieving those goals.

.44 One of the goals is titled "Results-Oriented Accountability for Grants." The overall goal is to maximize the value of grant funding by applying a risk-based, data-driven framework that balances compliance requirements with demonstrating successful results for the American taxpayer. This goal focuses on the following areas:

- Standardize data
  - — Identify, open, standardize, and link critical data sets to power analytics to enhance financial stewardship, performance management, and accountability.
- Digital tools to manage risk
  - — Use digital tools to modernize antiquated form-based compliance processes to assess and manage risk.
- Risk-based performance management
  - — Leverage existing data such as those produced by annual audits of recipients to drive a risk-based framework for performance management that drives results.

.45 As part of this goal, OMB, the Department of Education, and the Department of Health and Human Services will establish a governance structure that ensures that all major grant-making agencies participate and contribute to the execution of the goal. Key milestones have been set and are tracked on a quarterly basis. An example of actions noted in the Q1 Action Plan was to issue a "skinny" 2018 *Compliance Supplement* to allow OMB additional time and resources to be able to streamline the 2019 *Compliance Supplement* to focus on compliance requirements that "inform performance." (Part of this goal was accomplished with the issuance of the 2018 *Compliance Supplement*.) Another milestone of the action plan is to "[s]elect programs to pilot flexibilities in agencies with strong risk management that ties in performance." Also listed is a goal to streamline the *Compliance Supplement* with "an increased focus on compliance requirements that affect performance." Links to the quarter tracking can be found at https://www.performance.gov/cap/cap_goal_8.html.

Federal Audit Clearinghouse

.46 The Federal Audit Clearinghouse (FAC) is in the process of updating the 2019 data collection form, which will first be effective for audits of fiscal years ending in 2019, and will be used for audits covering fiscal periods ending in 2019, 2020, and 2021. At the time of this writing, the final revisions are not yet known because the FAC is still analyzing comments received in response to a *Federal Register* notice that proposed changes to the data collection form. Based on that *Federal Register* notice, there were four main changes being considered as follows:

- Audit finding information currently required to be included in the form by auditors would be expanded to include the actual text of each audit finding.
- Auditors would be asked to indicate whether a communication such as a management letter was issued.
- Auditees would be required to include the text of their corrective action plan.
- Auditees would also be required to include the text of the notes to the schedule of expenditures of federal awards.

.47 Additionally, the notice proposed that nonfederal entities that will not meet the threshold requiring submission of a single audit report be allowed to voluntarily notify the FAC that they did not meet the reporting threshold. The notice also proposes that any voluntarily provided information in this regard would be posted to the FAC.

.48 It is possible that not all changes noted here will be found in the final revision. Auditors should watch for the final revisions to the data collection form and submission process to begin understanding them for their 2019 single audits.

> Note that for 2018 audits there are no changes to the data collection form or FAC submission process. Also, when writing your audit reports and findings, keep in mind that the reporting packages submitted to the FAC are now publicly available.

Department of Education Update

.49 The Department of Education (Education) previously had a requirement (established through several Federal Student Aid [FSA] memorandums) for institutions participating in Title IV programs to notify their School Participation Division if the Student Financial Aid (SFA) cluster was not to be audited as a major program because it met the criteria in the Uniform Guidance for a low-risk program. Education issued an updated FSA memorandum dated March 29, 2018 stating that institutions participating in Title IV programs that submit a single audit that does not include the SFA cluster as a major program will no longer be required to notify their respective School Participation Division of the low-risk assessments. The memorandum reminds institutions that they must still submit (via the eZ-Audit system) their complete single audit each year by the due date regardless of whether the SFA cluster was audited as a major program. Finally, it states that the impact on year three testing requirements (after two years of low-risk assessments) for fiscal year (FY) 2019 audits and beyond is still under review. The memorandum is available at https://ifap.ed.gov/eannouncements/032918singleauditsubrequirefiscalyrendwithincalyr2018.html.

Housing and Urban Development Update

.50 The Department of Housing and Urban Development (HUD) is at various stages of making needed updates to its hard-coded electronic agreed-upon procedures engagement (AUP) report templates. These updates are needed to reflect report wording revisions resulting from the issuance of the AICPA's clarified attestation standards, which, for AUP engagements, were effective for AUP reports dated on or after May 1, 2017.

.51 The entities subject to HUD's AUP requirement include public housing agencies (PHAs) subject to single audit requirements, as well as multifamily housing programs and lenders subject to an audit under HUD's *Consolidated Audit Guide*. In each case, the required AUP engagement involves the practitioner comparing an auditee's electronically submitted financial and compliance information to the related hard copy supporting documentation and then issuing an electronic AUP report template via the relevant HUD submission system. Practitioners do not have the ability to revise HUD's AUP report template wording.

.52 At this time, the AUP templates for PHAs and multifamily housing programs have been updated. However, on the lender side, HUD staff have informed GAQC staff that the hard-coded electronic AUP report templates used for submissions in the Lender Electronic Assessment Portal (LEAP) have not yet been updated to reflect the report wording requirements of the clarified attestation standards. No date been given concerning the timing of a future update.

.53 After consulting with the AICPA's Audit and Assurance staff, the GAQC offers the following advice for practitioners performing lender audits as it relates to the required HUD AUP engagement and the out-of-date AUP report templates. Practitioners are advised to proceed with clicking "Submit" to process the electronic AUP reports in LEAP so that auditees are able to meet their submission requirement. However, the GAQC also recommends that practitioners issue a separate AUP report that reflects the requirements of the clarified attestation standards for AUP engagements and provide it to the client. Being able to support that an AUP report was issued in accordance with the standards will assist practitioners in the event the AUP engagement is selected as part of an internal inspection process, a peer review, or a federal quality control review.

USDA Rural Development Update

.54 If you perform engagements for for-profit rural development (RD) multifamily housing entities, you should be aware that on November 24, 2017, the U.S. Department of Agriculture (USDA) Rural Housing Service (RHS) published a final rule, "Multi-Family Housing Program Requirements to Reduce Financial Reporting Requirements," which revises the financial reporting requirements for RD multifamily housing. The final rule aligns RD reporting requirements with those of HUD and is effective for borrowers for fiscal years beginning on or after January 1, 2018 (see following discussion of follow-up guidance issued by USDA clarifying the effective date).

.55 The revised RD requirements require a compliance audit using HUD's *Consolidated Audit Guide* (with certain modifications for RD projects) for for-profit borrowers receiving $500,000 or more in combined federal financial assistance and removes requirements for an AUP engagement. The final rule notes that Section 514 and Section 515 proposals for new developments are still subject to an AUP engagement set forth in 7 CFR 3560.72(b). Additionally, the final rule adds three new certifications for borrowers.

.56 RHS issued a follow-up Unnumbered Letter (UL) on January 24, 2018, to clarify that the reporting change will not affect 2017 reporting requirements except to eliminate the AUP requirement for the FY 2017 reporting cycle when a borrower submits a statement that requests the elimination of the AUP engagement for the FY 2017 reporting cycle. The UL provides an example statement that an entity could make, which must be for a single project and can be made by email or written correspondence prior to or with the year-end reports. The UL also indicates that the reporting change will be optional for FY 2018 and mandatory starting in FY 2019.

.57 State and local governments, Indian tribes, and not-for-profit organizations (nonfederal entities) with combined federal assistance of $750,000 or more are not affected by this final rule or the UL, as they are required to have a single audit. Nonfederal entities receiving less than $750,000 in combined federal financial assistance will continue to submit owner-certified prescribed forms as clarified in the UL.

.58 The UL also provides guidance on what is included in combined federal financial assistance for both for-profit borrowers and nonfederal entities. It also notes that further guidance on FY 2018 year-end reporting requirements, along with revisions to chapter 4, "Account Servicing," of RD Handbook HB-3-3560, *MFH Project Servicing Handbook*, as well additional training, will be issued at a later time.

Catalog of Federal Domestic Assistance

.59 Information previously found on cfda.gov, the former Catalog of Federal Domestic Assistance (CFDA) website, has been moved to a new website. If you attempt to access cfda.gov, you are automatically redirected to https://beta.sam.gov, which is now the official source of assistance listings. It includes a comprehensive description of all federal assistance, including information on eligibility, how to apply, and matching requirements.

.60 This is part of a larger effort by the General Services Administration to merge 10 current websites related to various aspects of federal acquisitions and awards into 1 website. To that end, the website also contains resources regarding contracts awarded under the FAR, which are described as "assistance awards" on the website. At September 2018, the website was being described as the official source of information regarding what was formerly on the CFDA website. However, a number of other original websites related to acquisitions will coexist with the beta.sam.gov website until they are retired. Examples of these websites are fbo.gov, fpds.gov, and wdol.gov. Once the websites are all retired, beta.sam.gov will be renamed "sam.gov."

Uniform Guidance Considerations

Uniform Guidance Frequently Asked Questions

.61 Subsequent to the issuance of the Uniform Guidance, a series of frequently asked questions (FAQs) on the Uniform Guidance were developed. As noted in the *Compliance Supplement*, the FAQs are meant to provide additional context, background, and clarification of the policies described in the Uniform Guidance and should be considered in the single audit work plan and reviews. The FAQs cover a wide variety of topics and are often referenced by both auditees and auditors. Access the latest version of the FAQs, which were last updated in July 2017, at https://cfo.gov/grants/uniform-guidance/. Each update of the FAQ document indicates which questions and answers are new or revised so that readers can quickly see which revisions have been made.

Corrective Action Plan and Summary Schedule of Prior Audit Findings

.62 Under the Uniform Guidance, the auditee is required to promptly follow up and take corrective action on audit findings. This includes the preparation of a corrective action plan (CAP) and a summary schedule of prior audit findings (SSPAF). These two documents are required parts of the reporting package submitted to the FAC. It is important that the auditor understand that the CAP and the SSPAF are the responsibility of the auditee, and that the auditor's actions around those documents reflect that. FAQ .511-1 states that that the auditor should not prepare these documents for the auditee and that the auditee must submit the corrective action plan on auditee letterhead. Although the FAQ does not specifically extend that requirement to the SSPAF, requesting that the auditee's SSPAF be placed on auditee letterhead would be consistent with FAQ question .511-1 and would more clearly delineate the schedule as an auditee-prepared document.

Government-Wide Audit Quality Study

.63 2 CFR 200.513 of the Uniform Guidance requires that a government-wide audit quality study be performed once every six years beginning in 2018 or at such other interval as determined by OMB, and it requires the results to be made public. The study is to determine the quality of single audits by providing a statistically reliable estimate of the extent that single audits conform to applicable requirements, standards, and procedures. This in turn may lead to recommendations to address noted quality issues, including recommendations for any changes to applicable requirements, standards, and procedures.

.64 FAQ 200.513-1 provides further clarification on the timing of the study. That FAQ states that the single audit quality project will examine single audit engagements performed under the Uniform Guidance that are submitted to the FAC no earlier than 2018. Therefore, it is expected that the examination of single audit engagements as part of the quality project may occur in 2019 or 2020, as determined by the OMB.

What Can Auditors Do to Enhance Audit Quality?

.65 One way to work on increasing the quality of audits performed is for auditors to educate themselves on the areas of a single audit that are known to be problem areas. This will assist auditors in establishing an effective system of quality control specific to the firm's governmental audit practice. An effectively designed and implemented quality control system will provide reasonable assurance that the firm and its personnel comply with professional standards and regulatory requirements and that proper reports are issued. There are a number of resources to assist with establishing an effective quality control system and in performing single audits, some of which are mentioned throughout this alert.

.66 AICPA Audit Guide Government Auditing Standards *and Single Audits* contains information on both the Yellow Book audit and the Uniform Guidance compliance audit, including example auditor reports. Other resources include various checklists available to assist in an audited entity's quality control system and for auditors reviewing single audit engagements. Both peer review and audit quality checklists and practice aids are available for this purpose. Also, the GAQC provides up-to-date information regarding single audits, along with a number of resources regarding audit quality for members. Furthermore, some agency inspector generals have checklists or audit manuals that an auditor may find useful.

.67 Although documentation and communication of policies and procedures related to the quality control system in smaller firms may be less formal and less extensive than in larger firms, staff should be knowledgeable about the quality control policies regarding the quality control system. The quality control systems related to a firm's single audit practice should focus on areas that have been shown to be problematic.

.68 An auditor can seek out information regarding areas of common deficiencies in a number of ways. One such way is the listing of audit deficiencies compiled by the AICPA Peer Review and Professional Ethics divisions. Additional staff training may be warranted in areas in which audit deficiencies are commonly found.

.69 Educate yourself. Look for resources where audit quality is discussed. Obtain appropriate CPE each year to help ensure competency. One excellent resource is the *AICPA Competency Framework: Governmental Auditing,* which is designed to help CPAs understand the knowledge and skills necessary to perform high-quality single audits. You can find additional information on the competency framework in paragraph .120 of this alert.

.70 Other actions could include the following:

- A proactive review of your firm's data collection form and reporting package submissions in the FAC
- Selection of an adequate cross section of governmental audits for engagement quality control review as part of your quality control system
- Selection of a peer reviewer who has adequate experience and knowledge in the type of governmental engagements your firm performs

.71 These reviews of your single audit engagements will assist in identifying problem areas where changes and adjustments need to be made to improve the quality of your single audits.

Audit and Attest Developments

Statement on Auditing Standards No. 133

.72 The Auditing Standards Board (ASB) issued Statement on Auditing Standards (SAS) No. 133, *Auditor Involvement With Exempt Offering Documents* (AU-C sec. 945), in 2017. SAS No. 133 does not amend or supersede any previous SAS. It is effective for exempt offering documents with which the auditor is involved that are initially distributed, circulated, or submitted on or after June 15, 2018.

.73 The primary objective in the development of SAS No. 133 was to establish standards-level requirements for when an auditor is involved with an exempt offering document and the procedures required when involved. Prior to the issuance of SAS No. 133, the AICPA provided best practice guidance on the auditor's responsibilities in municipal securities offerings through industry-specific auditing guidance appearing in the AICPA Audit and Accounting Guides *State and Local Governments*, *Health Care Entities*, and *Not-for-Profit Entities* (AICPA guides). In developing SAS No. 133, the ASB broadened the scope of the project to address auditor involvement with offerings of all securities exempt from registration under the Securities Act of 1933, as amended, and to franchise offerings.

.74 Auditors that previously followed the best practice guidance contained in the AICPA guides relating to municipal securities offerings will likely not see a significant impact on their practice due to SAS No. 133. However, there are some differences between the guidance in SAS No. 133 and the best practice guidance. One difference is that the scope of SAS No. 133 is broader than just municipal securities offerings. Examples of the types of offerings now covered by the SAS include the following:

- Securities issued by not-for-profit religious, education, or charitable organizations
- Crowdfunding
- Small issues of securities (for example, Regulation A offerings)
- Franchise offerings

.75 In addition, the SAS modifies the activities (also referred to as triggers) establishing auditor involvement. Both SAS No. 133 and best practice guidance assume the auditor's report on the financial statements is included in the related offering. Finally, the SAS clarifies what an auditor is required to do when involved in an offering. The best practice guidance in the AICPA guides broadly directed the auditor to the procedures in AU-C section 720, *Other Information in Documents Containing Audited Financial Statements*. SAS No. 133 continues to point the auditor to AU-C section 720; however, it specifies that the auditor should apply paragraphs .06.18. The SAS also adds a new requirement for the auditor to perform procedures designed to identify events occurring between the date of the auditor's report and the date of the distribution, circulation, or submission of the exempt offering document that, had they been known to the auditor as of the date of the auditor's report, may have caused the auditor to revise the auditor's report.

Enhancing Audit Quality Initiative

.76 The CPA profession is highly regarded for its commitment to excellence and protection of the public. In the face of increased business complexity, we must strive to continue providing quality services. As a result, the AICPA launched the Enhancing Audit Quality (EAQ) initiative in May 2014 and published *Enhancing Audit Quality — A 6-Point Plan to Improve Audits* in May 2015. In addition to reports published in 2016 and 2017, a report titled "Enhancing Audit Quality: 2018 Mid-Year Progress Report," is available at https://www.aicpa.org/interestareas/peerreview/eaq/eaq-annual-highlights-and-progress-reports.html.

.77 Work continues to be done in this area. The goal is to align the objectives of all audit-related AICPA efforts to improve audit performance. For more information and resources, visit the EAQ website at www.aicpa.org/interestareas/peerreview/pages/eaq.aspx.

.78 One risk area that has been identified as part of the initiative is single audits. To assist in enhancing audit quality, single audits have been designated as a peer review area of focus. As part of this initiative, the AICPA Peer Review Program did a study of potential quality factors in single audits. That study found a correlation between three factors and the conformity to professional standards. An infographic is available that shows the results and recommendations. A summary of those three factors and the results are as follows:

1. *Practice makes perfect.* The more single audits a firm performed every year (regardless of firm size), the more likely a given single audit was to conform to professional standards.
   a. One single audit performed — 38% conformity
   b. Two to 10 single audits performed — 51% conformity
   c. Eleven or more single audits performed — 85% conformity
2. *Commitment to quality.* GAQC members had a rate of conformity to professional standards two times greater than that of nonmembers.

> GAQC members that performed 11 or more single audits annually had a 100% conformity rate.

3. *Qualified engagement partners.* The higher the number of single audits the engagement partner performed annually, the higher the conformity.
   a. One single audit performed annually — 32% conformity
   b. Two to 10 single audits performed annually — 56% conformity
   c. Eleven or more single audits performed annually — 75% conformity

Enhancing Audit Quality — Single Audit Analysis

.79 As part of the EAQ initiative, a single audit analysis was done to identify those areas of single audit nonconformity that were most pervasive and to attempt to identify why the nonconformity occurred. As part of the analysis, examples of deficiencies were found, and auditor misconceptions were identified. These misconceptions may play a significant part in the quality of work.

.80 It was found that both auditors and peer reviewers appeared to be making inappropriate connections between the single audit and the financial statement audit. Some misconceptions found include the following:

- Multiple auditors believed it was appropriate to rely on a walk-through of internal control over financial reporting to eliminate the need for testing controls over compliance.

- Several auditors believed, consistent with a financial statement audit, that by assessing control risk at "high," they could eliminate the need to test controls over compliance.
- Several auditors performed tests of details as part of their financial statement audit, doing no work to assess compliance with direct and material requirements, and classified the procedures as "dual-purpose tests" (forgoing any compliance testing).

.81 The items noted here are misconceptions because the Uniform Guidance requires the auditor to perform procedures to obtain an understanding of internal control over federal programs sufficient to plan the audit to support a low assessed level of control risk of noncompliance for major programs. Furthermore, testing of both internal control over compliance and testing of compliance with direct and material compliance requirements for each major program is required in a Uniform Guidance compliance audit.

.82 These misconceptions indicate that some auditors do not understand the fact that a Uniform Guidance compliance audit is a separate audit of compliance with its own requirements. The content that follows presents some deficiencies found in the areas of planning, internal control testing, and compliance testing, and misconceptions related to those deficiencies.

Planning the Single Audit

.83

Examples of deficiencies related to single audit planning
Indicated an applicable compliance requirement was not direct and material, but didn't document rationale
No evidence in the file that the auditor considered which compliance requirements were direct and material
Failed to assess risk of material noncompliance due to fraud
Lack of evidence to support the determination that the auditee has met the criteria to be considered "low risk"
Missed compliance requirements by using out-of-date *Compliance Supplement*
Missed compliance requirements by failing to consider the *Compliance Supplement*

Misconceptions

- Other
    - Believed a "Y" in the matrix of compliance requirements in the *Compliance Supplement* meant that a requirement "could" apply, and that documentation when the requirement did not apply was not required
    - Believed that, when a single audit is not required but is requested by the client, the firm could forgo certain required procedures while still being able to issue the same reports

- — Believed following a third-party practice aid was an appropriate alternative to considering the *Compliance Supplement*
- — Believed they only needed to follow the guidance included in Part 4 of the *Compliance Supplement* and not the suggested audit procedures in Part 3
- — Believed including the grant agreement in the audit file eliminated the need to document the determination of what is direct and material

Controls Testing in a Single Audit

.84

Examples of deficiencies related to internal control testing
Insufficient evidence in file that the firm tested controls around each major program's direct and material compliance requirements
Failed to document understanding of controls for each major program's direct and material compliance requirements
No evidence that the firm tested controls over compliance at all

Misconceptions

- Most common
  - — Thought a walk-through of internal controls over financial reporting was sufficient to eliminate the need for testing of controls over compliance
  - — "Power-ticked" generic audit programs, signing off on procedures for which there was no indication that work was performed
  - — Could orally explain their understanding of internal control but did not document it
- Other
  - — Thought it was permissible to perform one high-level internal control assessment and apply that to all major programs (without addressing each direct and material compliance requirement)
  - — Used a generic questionnaire that was not tailored to the client
  - — Relied on controls at the grantor to eliminate the need for control testing
  - — Relied heavily on audit programs without understanding the steps they were signing off on
  - — Thought no testing of controls was permissible when "100% of disbursements were tested"
  - — Did not test controls because "federal awards follow the same internal control system as nonfederal awards"

- — Did not test controls, thinking such tests are required every three years
- — Did not test controls because they assessed control risk at "high"
- — Believed the auditor could rely on compliance testing to eliminate the need for control testing
- — Lacked an understanding of the difference between control and compliance testing
- — Peer reviewer believed the failure to document an understanding of internal control over compliance was permissible because the auditee was smaller and less complex
- — Believed control risk can be assessed at "low" without any testing of controls over compliance

Compliance Testing in a Single Audit

.85

Examples of deficiencies related to compliance testing
Insufficient evidence that the firm tested each major program's direct and material compliance requirements
Insufficient documentation of the sufficiency of the sample or how it was selected
No evidence that the firm tested compliance at all
Performed financial statement audit procedures (for example, traced invoices to the general ledger in lieu of compliance audit procedures)

Misconceptions

- Most common
  - — Performed common financial reporting tests of details instead of compliance tests
  - — Did not understand that the single audit is a separate audit of compliance that needs its own planning, risk assessment, materiality determination, and so on
  - — Misunderstood the meaning and purpose of dual-purpose testing
- Other
  - — Thought cash management was not applicable because "funds were received only after they were incurred"
  - — Believed compliance testing was unnecessary because the auditee's operation "was small and simple" in nature and there was adequate work done as part of the financial statement audit
  - — Believed a test of transactions for financial statement purposes is a "dual-purpose test," in that the test can be

relied upon for the financial statement and compliance audit (Note: Test did not address direct and material compliance requirements, but rather tested financial statement assertions and traced total activity back to the trial balance.)

.86 As evidenced by these misconceptions, some auditors performing single audits are lacking a basic understanding of requirements and guidance related to a single audit. As part of efforts to enhance audit quality, resources have been developed to assist the auditor. Several of those resources are referenced throughout this alert. In addition, one practice aid available is *Establishing and Maintaining a System of Quality Control for a CPA Firm's Accounting and Auditing Practice*. One version has been developed for small- and medium-sized firms, and one for sole practitioners. Visit www.aicpa.org/interestareas/frc/pages/enhancingauditqualitypracticeaid.aspx to access the right one for you.

Ethics Update

Ethics — Frequently Asked Question, March 2018

.87 The AICPA Professional Ethics Division released an FAQ in March 2018 entitled "Long association of senior personnel of the engagement team."[5] Question 1 of the FAQ asks: "Does the familiarity threat to independence increase when senior personnel of the engagement team have been on the attest engagement team for a long time?" *Senior personnel* referred to for this purpose are defined as partners, partner equivalents, and any other individuals on the attest engagement team who have responsibility for decision-making on significant matters that affect the results of the attest engagement and who maintain regular contact with attest client management or those charged with governance.

.88 The FAQ notes that the familiarity threat to independence may increase when senior personnel serve on the team for a long time. Senior personnel should determine the significance of these factors in order to evaluate the threat to independence. Examples of factors related to both the senior personnel on the engagement and the attest client that may need to be considered are provided.

.89 Question 2 of the FAQ asks whether the firm can still perform the attest engagement if it is determined there is a significant familiarity threat. The FAQ notes that if safeguards can be applied to eliminate the threat, or reduce it to an acceptable level, the firm could continue to perform the engagement. Examples of some possible safeguards are provided. Any threats and safeguards applied should be documented. If safeguards cannot be applied to eliminate the threat or reduce it to an acceptable level, independence would be impaired.

Ethics Interpretation — Data Hosting

.90 The Professional Ethics Executive Committee (PEEC) adopted an interpretation, "Hosting Services," (ET sec. 1.295.143) under the "Independence Rule" (ET sec. 1.200.001).[6] Under that interpretation, independence will be

---

[5] https://www.aicpa.org/interestareas/professionalethics/resources/tools/downloadabledocuments/ethics-general-faqs.pdf

[6] All ET sections can be found in AICPA *Professional Standards*.

impaired when a member CPA takes responsibility for maintaining internal control over an attest client's data or records. Examples given include a scenario in which the CPA assumes responsibility for safeguarding the information by agreeing to do the following:

- Be the sole host of a client's financial or nonfinancial information system
- Be the custodian for the client's data such that the client's data are incomplete and accessible only through the CPA
- Provide business continuity or disaster recovery services to the client

.91 A basic precept in the independence rules is that CPAs should not perform activities that are management's responsibilities. This interpretation interprets hosting services to mean that the CPA has accepted responsibility for maintaining internal control over an attest client's information, thereby impairing independence. See the interpretation for complete information. The interpretation was originally set to be effective September 1, 2018. However, the effective date has been extended to July 1, 2019, to allow AICPA members adequate time to implement any necessary changes resulting from the new interpretation.

Peer Review Update

.92 The AICPA peer review team issued a June 2018 Reviewer Alert (reviewer alert) designed to alert peer reviewers to potential challenges faced by auditors performing engagements under *Government Auditing Standards* and single audits for the purpose of assisting peer reviewers in performing peer reviews of those engagements. These engagements are subject to quality control reviews and desk reviews performed by federal cognizant and oversight agencies. In addition, increased scrutiny of these engagements is likely due to the future study of audit quality required by the Uniform Guidance.

.93 Peer reviewers are focusing on common problem areas, and auditors may want to take a second look at them in their practice. Though these are not the only areas of focus for peer reviewers, the topics discussed here include the following:

- Yellow Book independence
- Compliance audits below the single audit threshold
- Single audit documentation
- Identification of high-risk type B programs

The discussion that follows uses information from the reviewer alert in identifying problem areas to help an audit organization focus on areas of single audit engagements that may be nonconforming.

Yellow Book Independence[7]

.94 The Yellow Book independence requirements build on the AICPA requirements related to auditor independence, especially related to documentation. As noted in the reviewer alert, *Government Auditing Standards* indicates

---

[7] This content, including paragraph references, is based on the 2011 Yellow Book, which are the standards in effect for peer reviews currently being performed.

the auditor is required to document the following when performing nonaudit services for attest engagements performed under GAGAS:

1. Document management's ability to oversee the nonaudit services to be provided via documentation of management's skills, knowledge, and expertise (SKE).
2. Document the auditor's understanding with the entity for which the auditor will perform nonaudit services, including:
   a. objectives of the nonaudit service,
   b. services to be performed,
   c. auditee's acceptance of its responsibilities,
   d. auditor's responsibilities, and
   e. any limitations of the nonaudit service. Paragraph .01*c* of the "General Requirements for Performing Nonattest Services" interpretation (ET sec. 1.295.040) indicates that this understanding should be documented before performing nonattest services.
3. Document significant threats to independence that require the application of safeguards, along with safeguards applied using the conceptual framework of paragraph 3.24 of *Government Auditing Standards*.

.95 It is noted that the failure of the auditor to document any of the three items should be evaluated independently, and documentation of all three must be satisfied to conform to the relevant professional standards. Documentation of fewer than all of the items is not sufficient. For example, even if there is evidence of the performance of a safeguard procedure and all the other required independence elements are present, documentation would be nonconforming if the auditor failed to document the understanding with the client of the nonaudit services to be performed.

.96 The reviewer alert notes that peer reviewers should evaluate whether the reviewed firm understands the independence and related documentation requirements. Peer reviewers should also remind the reviewed firm that the response to any material departures from Yellow Book independence standards should focus on remediation of the steps that were not previously performed or not documented.

Financial Statement Preparation as a Significant Threat to Independence

.97 GAO has indicated that financial statement preparation, except in rare circumstances (for example, very limited auditor involvement), should generally be considered a significant threat to independence. Although not officially stated in the 2011 Yellow Book, practitioners and widely used third-party practice aids for Yellow Book engagements often consider financial statement preparation as a significant threat to independence. Therefore, peer reviewers should carefully evaluate whether self-review threats have been properly considered if the reviewed firm (auditor) prepares the audited entity's financial statements. Note that the 2018 Yellow Book clearly states that financial statement preparation creates a significant threat to independence when the auditor prepares the statements in their entirety from a client-provided trial balance or underlying accounting records. See the discussion beginning at paragraph .12 of this publication for more information.

Compliance Audits Below the Single Audit Threshold

.98 There are potential implications that should be considered by peer reviewers if an auditor performed an audit following the requirements of the Uniform Guidance (or other applicable guidance) when the auditee's total federal expenditures are less than $750,000 (or other applicable threshold). Although there are cases in which the audited entity (auditee) requests the compliance audit even though not required, the concern is that the auditor performing the audit did not understand the requirements, or did not respond appropriately to changed circumstances.

.99 Attempting to perform a single audit for an auditee that is not technically subject to the Uniform Guidance creates a number of complications that should be considered, such as the following:

1. Certain aspects of the audit may not be applicable as defined in the Uniform Guidance, such as
   a. the major program determination steps and thresholds (for example, the type A/B program threshold is based on an entity having $750,000 or more of federal expenditures), and
   b. submission of the audit to the FAC (2 CFR 200.512 of Subpart F of the Uniform Guidance).
2. Several aspects of the OMB *Compliance Supplement*, other guidance, and practice aids may not be applicable.
3. The auditor's single audit reporting may be misleading if not appropriately modified (for example, the title of the report and the statement in the body of the report that the audit was performed in accordance with the Uniform Guidance).
4. The auditee should consider that audit costs for entities that are exempted from having a single audit under Uniform Guidance because federal expenditures are less than $750,000 are not an allowable federal expenditure eligible for reimbursement (2 CFR 200.425 of Subpart E of the Uniform Guidance).
5. The compliance audit performed will not qualify the auditee as a low-risk auditee under the Uniform Guidance in the subsequent year as the audit was not technically performed in accordance with the Uniform Guidance, which includes submission of the data collection form and reporting package to the FAC (2 CFR 200.520 of Subpart F of the Uniform Guidance).
6. The testing of a program as a "major program" will not count toward the two-year look back for program risk assessment purposes in subsequent years' major program determination.

.100 The reviewer alert notes that if the reviewed firm (auditor) issues a report stating that a single audit was performed under the Uniform Guidance, but total federal expenditures are less than the Uniform Guidance threshold and a specific program audit was not required by the governmental agency, the peer reviewer should obtain a clear understanding of the auditor's considerations. An auditor's failure to do any of the following is considered a material departure from professional standards that would cause the engagement to be deemed nonconforming for peer review purposes:

- Make appropriate considerations of relevant factors.

- Document significant conclusions for the application of or departure from professional standards and applicable legal and regulatory requirements (paragraphs .02 and .08 of AU-C section 230, *Statement of Cash Flows*).
- Issue appropriately tailored auditor's reports when a single audit was not required.

Single Audit Documentation

.101 Deficiencies related to single audit documentation are commonly found. Key single audit documentation deficiencies that warrant attention from peer reviewers include the following:

- Auditor does not document the rationale for concluding that an applicable compliance requirement was not direct and material and thus not tested.
- Auditor does not properly document the understanding of internal controls over each direct and material compliance requirement for each major program.
- Auditor does not properly document testing of internal controls over each direct and material compliance requirement.
- Auditor does not specifically assess and document the risk of material noncompliance with each major program's compliance requirement occurring due to fraud.
- Auditor does not perform or properly document testing of compliance over each direct and material compliance requirement.
- Auditor does not document consideration of controls surrounding preparation of the schedule of expenditures of federal awards (SEFA) or procedures used to determine that the SEFA was presented fairly in relation to the financial statements as a whole.

Identifying High-Risk Type B Programs

.102 A frequent issue that has been noted during peer reviews and oversights includes the auditor's failure to test as major all high-risk type B programs that have been identified by the auditor. The Uniform Guidance explicitly requires that all identified high-risk type B programs be audited as major programs (2 CFR 200.518(e)(2)). For example, if it is determined that the nonfederal entity has 10 low-risk type A programs, an auditor needs to perform risk assessments until 3 type B programs have been identified as high risk (¼ or 25% of the number of low-risk type A programs, rounded up). Therefore, if the first 3 type B programs assessed are identified as high risk, the auditor can stop there. If the first program assessed is identified as low risk and the next 3 programs assessed are identified as high risk, the auditor can stop there (4 programs assessed). But if the auditor conducted risk assessments on all 10 type B programs and identified 7 in the working papers as high risk, the auditor is required to audit all 7 as major programs. Note that risk assessments of type B programs are not required if there are no low-risk type A programs. Note also that the auditor is only required to perform risk assessments on type B programs that exceed 25% of the determined type A threshold.

Emphasis Point

The Uniform Guidance states that the auditor is not required to identify more high-risk type B programs than at least one-fourth the number of type A programs identified as low risk. It is possible to risk assess all of an auditee's type B programs and determine that fewer than one-fourth the number of low-risk type A programs are high-risk type B programs, or that none are high-risk type B programs. However, the Uniform Guidance does require all identified high-risk type B programs to be audited as a major program.

.103 Peer reviewers are reminded to consider whether the audit documentation supports the auditor's performance of required type B risk assessments when the auditor has identified low-risk type A programs and whether all identified high-risk type B programs are tested as major.

Practice Aid — Yellow Book Independence

.104 The AICPA developed the *2011 Yellow Book Independence — Nonaudit Services Documentation Practice Aid* to assist auditors in meeting the requirements of the 2011 revision of the Yellow Book. Currently, the AICPA is in the process of updating this practice aid for the 2018 Yellow Book and it is expected to be available in early 2019. In the meantime, if you are performing an audit under the 2011 Yellow Book, this practice aid can help in identifying and evaluating threats to independence when considering whether to provide a nonaudit service. The following are some key features of the practice aid:

- A step-by-step questionnaire template that covers the thought process and related auditor documentation considerations when evaluating independence
- Detailed appendixes that include, among other things, real-life examples of actual nonaudit service scenarios and how an auditor might respond to them
- Information on how an auditor might consider an auditee's skills, knowledge, or experience, which is a requirement for every nonaudit service provided
- An illustrative completed version of the questionnaire template

On the Horizon

.105 The FAC is in the process of updating the 2019 data collection form. See the earlier section titled "Federal Audit Clearinghouse" for information regarding expected changes. Auditors should watch for these changes to assist in preparing for 2019 single audit submissions. In addition, auditors should be alert to the possibility of revisions to, or clarifications of, the Uniform Guidance made through technical corrections or FAQs. Also, federal agencies may issue communications related to audits of their federal programs. The GAQC is an excellent resource for that information.

.106 Auditors should keep abreast of accounting developments and upcoming guidance that may affect their engagements. Information on, and copies of, outstanding exposure drafts may be obtained from the various standard setters' websites. These websites contain in-depth information about proposed standards and other projects in the pipeline.

AICPA GAQC

.107 The GAQC is a voluntary membership center for CPA firms and state audit organizations (SAOs) designed to improve the quality of governmental audits. For the purposes of the GAQC, governmental audits are performed under GAGAS and are audits and attestation engagements of federal, state, or local governments; not-for-profit entities; and certain for-profit organizations such as housing projects and colleges and universities that participate in governmental programs or receive governmental financial assistance.

.108 The mission of the GAQC is as follows:

- To raise awareness about the importance of governmental audits
- To serve as a comprehensive resource provider on governmental audits for member firms and SAOs
- To create a community of firms and SAOs that demonstrates a commitment to governmental audit quality
- To list member firms and SAOs to enable purchasers of governmental audit services to identify GAQC members
- To provide information about the GAQC's activities to other governmental audit stakeholders

.109 The GAQC keeps members informed about the latest developments through a number of resources such as tools and information to help members better manage their audit practices. CPA firms and SAOs that join the GAQC demonstrate their commitment to audit quality by agreeing to adhere to certain membership requirements.

.110 The GAQC has been in existence since September 2004. Since its launch, center membership has grown to over 2,000 member firms and 33 SAOs. The CPA firm members of the GAQC account for over 94 percent of the total federal expenditures covered in single audits found in the FAC (https://harvester.census.gov/facweb/) for the year 2016 (the latest year with complete submission data). The GAQC's focus is to promote the highest quality audits and save members time by providing a centralized place to find the information they need when they need it, to maximize quality and practice success.

.111 Center resources and benefits include the following:

- Email alerts with the latest audit and regulatory developments, including information on the revisions relating to the Uniform Guidance
- Exclusive webcasts and webinars on compliance auditing and timely topics relevant to governmental financial statement audits (Optional CPE is available for a small fee, and events are archived online.)
- Dedicated GAQC area on aicpa.org with resources, community events, products, and a complete listing of GAQC members in each state

- Single audit practice aids and tools, including a new tool to assist auditors in using the 2018 and 2017 *Compliance Supplements* together (see earlier section)
- Web events on topics relevant to single audits
- Auditee Resource Center containing practice aids and other resources to keep auditees well informed about audit requirements and other issues related to their audits
- GASB Matters page, which lists resources found on the website related to GASB topics of current interest
- Advocacy regarding issues related to the audit and regulatory environment facing auditors
- A marketing tool kit for member firms
- Savings on professional liability insurance

.112 Although some of the GAQC's resources are available only to members, other resources such as the Auditee Resource Center are available to the public and can be accessed from the GAQC website. For more information about the GAQC, visit www.aicpa.org/gaqc.

Help Desk: To enroll or learn more about the GAQC, including details on the membership requirements and fees and for a preview of member benefits, go to the membership page of the GAQC at www.aicpa.org/interestareas/governmentalauditquality/membership.html or email the GAQC staff at GAQC@aicpa.org.

GAQC Executive Committee

.113 The GAQC is governed by an executive committee that establishes general center policies and oversees its activities. The executive committee also establishes center membership requirements, subject to AICPA board of directors approval. Members of the executive committee must be members of the AICPA. For more information, visit the GAQC Executive Committee page at www.aicpa.org/interestareas/governmentalauditquality/community/pages/governmental%20audit%20quality%20executive%20committee.aspx.

AICPA GAQC Auditee Resource Center

.114 As noted earlier, the GAQC offers an Auditee Resource Center, which is open to the public and is intended for procurers of audit services (auditees). Information found in this section of the GAQC website relates to auditees that are required to undergo audits performed under GAGAS. Those audits include financial statement audits of governments and not-for-profit entities; Yellow Book audits; and compliance audits, including audits performed under the Uniform Guidance (referred to as single audits), HUD audits, and other compliance audits of for-profit entities.

.115 Although auditors are ultimately responsible for providing high-quality audit services, the GAQC recognizes that auditees play a key role in the audit process and are an important factor in the audit quality equation.

Well-informed auditees with strong governance structures increase the likelihood of high-quality audits and more efficient audits. Why might that be? Experience has shown that these auditees generally spend more time considering the qualifications of a potential auditor during the hiring process and evaluating the reasonableness of an auditor's anticipated hours in relation to the proposed fee based on the work to be performed. Further, these auditees have a stronger understanding about the audit requirements that apply to them, are better prepared for their audits, and more clearly understand their role in the audit process.

.116 To assist auditees with the audit process, the Auditee Resource Center includes information, tools, practice aids, and other resources that should be of interest and benefit to auditees. For example, there is an entire web page dedicated to Uniform Guidance considerations for auditees. Auditors should let their clients know about this resource.

.117 Access the Auditee Resource Center at www.aicpa.org/interestareas/governmentalauditquality/resources/auditeeresourcecenter/pages/default.aspx.

.118 Access the Auditee Resource Center Uniform Guidance resources at https://www.aicpa.org/InterestAreas/GovernmentalAuditQuality/Resources/AuditeeResourceCenter/Pages/SingleAuditToolsPracticeAidsandOtherResourcesforAuditees.aspx.

AICPA Single Audit Certificate Programs

.119 As part of the AICPA's EAQ initiative, the AICPA is offering exam-based intermediate and advanced level certificates to CPAs who perform single audits. The AICPA developed these certificate programs to help auditors demonstrate their level of expertise and commitment to excellence and distinguish themselves in the marketplace. The certificate programs may also assist those requiring a single audit in selecting a qualified and competent auditor. Since launching in 2016, over 450 single audit certificate digital badges have been awarded and viewed over 700,000 times by employers, clients, prospective clients, and peers.

.120 The single audit certificates, which are offered at the intermediate and advanced competency levels, are based on the Uniform Guidance and the *AICPA Competency Framework: Governmental Auditing*, with a focus on practice areas where deficiencies are commonly found. Both the intermediate and advanced certificate programs offer flexible learning options. Though the CPE courses offered are not required in order to take the exam, both the intermediate and advanced courses allow you to take CPE learning focusing on the areas covered in the certificate exams. Participants are not required to take the intermediate exam in order to take the advanced exam. Once you have successfully passed the exam (or exams), you will receive a digital badge that can be used across the internet to demonstrate your competency at either an intermediate or advanced level. The single audit certificates are available at http://sacert.aicpastore.com.

AICPA Not-for-Profit Initiatives

.121 The mission of each not-for-profit (NFP) may be unique, but NFPs share many common concerns around financial reporting, tax, audit, and governance. To meet the increasing needs in this fast-growing sector, the AICPA launched the following initiatives in 2015 that provide news, education, training, and resources to individuals who are CPAs and non-CPA professionals serving NFPs:

- Not-for-Profit Section
- Not-for-Profit Certificate Program

NFP Member Section

.122 In May 2015, the AICPA launched a membership section for practitioners and others who serve or work for the nation's growing NFP sector. The AICPA's Not-for-Profit Section (NFP section) provides support and resources in the areas of audit, financial accounting, and tax for members and other finance professionals. Though some content is accessible only by NFP section members, other content is available for use by the public. Visit www.aicpa.org/interestareas/notforprofit for more information or to join.

NFP Certificate Programs

.123 The AICPA offers two certificate programs for NFP professionals. These programs are available to anyone with an interest in learning more about financial management of NFPs.

Not-for-Profit Certificate

.124 The Not-for-Profit Certificate Program is specially designed to help accountants and others build the knowledge needed to gain a basic understanding of these entities and to support them in the pursuit of their mission. The Not-for-Profit Certificate program provides a foundation in NFP accounting, tax compliance, governance, and assurance. This online program is available on demand and offers 40 hours of CPE-eligible credit that is divided among 24 courses, delivered in 3 topical tracks.

.125 Participants learn about generally accepted accounting principles (GAAP) reporting standards that apply to NFPs, including financial statement presentation and disclosure requirements, state and federal filing requirements for tax-exempt organizations, best practices in board governance, financial oversight, internal controls, fraud and other risks, and audit planning considerations. Courses are available for purchase individually or as a package. All 24 courses must be completed to receive the certificate; however, there may be individual courses from which staff and volunteers can benefit. Learn more at www.aicpastore.com.

Not-for-Profit Certificate II

.126 Launched in December 2015, this 30-hour CPE program comprises 17 courses that build on the core principles presented in the first NFP certificate program; however, there is no required course of study before taking these courses. This online, video-based program is presented by leading NFP industry experts and is intended to teach participants to apply skills in a real-world setting. Participants learn how to prepare financial statements, how to complete IRS Form 990, how to build complex budgets, how to perform risk assessments, how to guide the strategic planning process, and how to work with an NFP's governing board. Learning exercises, targeted case studies, and detail-rich interpretations are interspersed throughout the video presentations. Courses are available for purchase individually or as a package and are accessible on demand. All 17 courses must be completed to receive the certificate; however, there may be individual courses from which staff and volunteers can benefit. Learn more at www.aicpastore.com.

Resource Central

.127 The following are various resources that practitioners who perform financial statement audits under *Government Auditing Standards* and compliance audits under the Uniform Guidance may find beneficial. Note that the AICPA Store has compiled a web page entitled "AICPA Governmental Guidance, Tools and Resources," which includes CPE, conferences, publications, and webcasts relevant to audits of state and local governments and NFPs, including *Government Auditing Standards* and single audit topics.

Publications

.128 Practitioners may find the following publications useful. Visit www.aicpastore.com and choose the format best for you — print, e-book, or online.

- Audit Guide Government Auditing Standards *and Single Audits* (2018) (product nos. AAGGAS18P [paperback], AAGGAS18E [e-book], or WRF-XX [online])
- Audit and Accounting Guide *Not-for-Profit Entities* (2018) (product nos. AAGNFP18P [paperback], AAGNFP18E [e-book], or WNP-XX [online])
- Audit and Accounting Guide *State and Local Governments* (2018) (product nos. AAGSLG18P [paperback], AAGSLG18E [e-book], or WGG-XX [online])
- Audit and Accounting Guide *Health Care Entities* (2018) (product nos. AAGHCO18P [paperback], AAGHCO18E [e-book], or WHC-XX [online])
- Audit Risk Alert *General Accounting and Auditing Developments — 2018/19* (product nos. ARAGEN18P [paperback], ARAGEN18E [e-book], or WGE-XX [online])
- Audit Risk Alert *Not-for-Profit Entities Industry Developments — 2018* (product nos. ARANFP18P [paperback], ARANFP18E [e-book], or WNP-XX [online])

Continuing Professional Education

.129 The AICPA offers a number of CPE courses that are valuable to CPAs working in public practice and industry, including many that are specifically related to audits performed under GAGAS and compliance audits performed under the Uniform Guidance. Visit www.aicpastore.com for a complete list of CPE courses.

Online CPE

.130 AICPA CPExpress, offered exclusively through the AICPA Store, is the AICPA's flagship online learning product. Divided into 1-credit and 2-credit courses that are available 24 hours a day, 7 days a week, AICPA CPExpress offers hundreds of hours of learning in a wide variety of topics. Subscriptions are available at www.aicpastore.com (product no. BYT-XX). Some topics of special interest to those performing single audits include the following:

- Single audits
- Uniform Guidance compliance audits
- Yellow Book requirements
- Accounting requirements for governments and NFP organizations
- Audit and accounting annual and quarterly updates on recent developments
- HUD-assisted projects
- Fraud detection and prevention

To register for individual courses or to learn more, visit www.aicpastore.com.

Webcasts

.131 Stay plugged in to what is happening and earn CPE credit right from your desktop. AICPA webcasts are high-quality CPE programs that bring you the latest topics from the profession's leading experts. Broadcast live, they allow you to interact with the presenters and join in the discussion. If you cannot make the live event, some webcasts are archived and available for viewing. For additional details on available webcasts, please visit www.aicpastore.com/ast/aicpa_cpa2biz_nav/responsive_top_nav/webcasts.jsp.

.132 The Webcast Pass is also available. With the annual Webcast Pass, you can explore a variety of topics specific to your current work or for future career opportunities: Choose courses from outside your required subject area and expand your knowledge at no additional cost. The Webcast Pass includes courses on accounting, auditing, fraud, tax, practice management, management accounting, and more.

Industry Conferences

.133 The AICPA sponsors three annual conferences that include a focus on *Government Auditing Standards* and Uniform Guidance topics that are held in the summer and fall of each year.

.134 The national AICPA Governmental Accounting and Auditing Update Conference (GAAC) is held each August in Washington, D.C. This conference is designed for CPAs working in federal, state, and local government; public practitioners performing single audits; and regulators who need to be aware of emerging developments. Attending this conference is a great way to receive timely information and guidance regarding federal, state, and local topics, along with practical advice on how to handle new legislation and standards from key government officials and representatives of the accounting profession, including the standard setters themselves.

.135 The national AICPA Governmental and Not-for-Profit Training Program is held in the fall each year. If you need hands-on training and are a CPA in public practice or a governmental or NFP staffer, then this conference is for you. You'll hear directly from the standard setters and industry leaders on a variety of topics, including developments in governmental accounting and auditing, financial statement reporting, and the latest in proposed regulations and laws on the local, state, and federal government levels, as well as developments affecting the NFP sector.

.136 The national AICPA Not-for-Profit Industry Conference is offered each June in Washington, D.C. The conference offers a wide range of topics geared toward both auditors and NFP professionals at every level: tax, management, audit and accounting, fund-raising, and regulatory.

.137 For further information about the conferences, call 888.777.7077 or visit www.aicpastore.com.

Member Service Center

.138 AICPA Member Service is committed to serving both members and customers of the AICPA who need assistance with membership, products, services, and activities. If you can't find what you are looking for or have a question that can't be answered by the information on one of our websites, please call the Member Service Center at 888.777.7077, Monday through Friday, 9 a.m. to 6 p.m. ET, or send an email to service@aicpa.org.

Government Accountability Office

.139 For technical or practice questions regarding the Yellow Book, please call 202.512.9535 or email yellowbook@gao.gov.

Accounting and Auditing Technical Hotline

.140 Do you have a complex technical question about GAAP, other comprehensive bases of accounting, or other technical matters? If so, use the AICPA's Accounting and Auditing Technical Hotline. AICPA staff will research your question and call you back with the answer. The hotline is available from 9 a.m. to 8 p.m. ET on weekdays. You can reach the Technical Hotline at 877.242.7212 or online at www.aicpa.org/research/technicalhotline/pages/default.aspx. Members can also email questions to aahotline@aicpa.org. Additionally, members can submit questions by completing a Technical Inquiry Form found on the same website.

Ethics Hotline

.141 In addition to the Technical Hotline, the AICPA also offers an Ethics Hotline. Members of the AICPA's Professional Ethics Team answer inquiries concerning independence and other behavioral issues related to the application of the AICPA Code of Professional Conduct. You can reach the Ethics Hotline at 888.777.7077 or by email at ethics@aicpa.org.

The Center for Plain English Accounting

.142 The Center for Plain English Accounting (CPEA) is a service available to Private Companies Practice Section (PCPS) member firms. The CPEA provides expertise and resources in a straightforward and clear style. Written responses to technical inquiries, webcasts on hot topics, and monthly reports and alerts help practitioners understand and implement the authoritative professional literature when auditing, reviewing, preparing, and compiling financial statements. To join the CPEA and take advantage of these valuable resources and guarantee your practice a seat at eight annual webcasts (16 CPE credits), go to www.aicpa.org/interestareas/centerforplainenglish accounting.

AICPA Online Professional Library: Accounting and Auditing Literature

.143 The AICPA has created your core accounting and auditing library online. The AICPA Online Professional Library is now customizable to suit your preferences or your firm's needs. You can also sign up for access to the entire library. Get access anywhere you can get online to FASB *Accounting Standards Codification*®; the AICPA's latest *Professional Standards*, *Technical Questions and Answers*, Audit and Accounting Guides, Audit Risk Alerts, Best Practices in Presentation and Disclosure publications; and more. To subscribe to this essential online service for accounting professionals, visit www.aicpastore.com.

Financial Reporting Center of AICPA.org

.144 CPAs face unprecedented changes in financial reporting. As such, the AICPA has created the Financial Reporting Center (FRC) to support you in the execution of high-quality financial reporting. The center provides exclusive members-only resources for the entire financial reporting process and can be accessed at www.aicpa.org/interestareas/frc/pages/default.aspx.

.145 The FRC provides timely and relevant news, guidance, and examples supporting the financial reporting process. You will find resources for accounting, preparing financial statements, and performing various types of engagements, including compilation and review, audit and attest, and assurance and advisory.

AICPA Industry Expert Panels

AICPA Industry Expert Panel — State and Local Government

.146 The State and Local Government Expert Panel is an AICPA volunteer group whose purpose is to identify state and local government financial reporting and auditing issues and to work with appropriate bodies for resolutions benefiting the public interest; conduct liaison activities with GASB, regulators such as the GAO and OMB, and applicable industry associations; and advise and assist in the development of AICPA products and services related to state and local government audits. For information about the activities of the State and Local Government Expert Panel, visit the panel's website in the "Industry Insights" section of the FRC at www.aicpa.org/interestareas/frc/industryinsights/pages/expert_panel_state_and_local_governments.aspx.

AICPA Industry Expert Panel — Not-for-Profit Entities

.147 The AICPA Not-for-Profit Entities Expert Panel assists those working in the industry by identifying financial reporting and auditing issues within the industry for which guidance from standard-setting bodies is needed and by working with appropriate bodies having authority over such standards in finding resolutions to issues. For more information about the activities of the Not-for-Profit Entities Expert Panel, visit the panel's website in the "Industry Insights" section of the FRC at www.aicpa.org/interestareas/frc/industryinsights/pages/expert_panel_not_for_profit_entities.aspx.

Industry Websites

.148 The internet covers a vast amount of information that may be valuable to auditors performing single audits, including current industry trends and developments. Some of the more relevant sites for auditors performing single audits include those shown in the following table.

Organization	*Website*
AICPA	aicpa.org www.aicpastore.com www.ifrs.com
AICPA Governmental Audit Quality Center	www.aicpa.org/InterestAreas/GovernmentalAuditQuality.html
AICPA Not-for-Profit Interest Area and Member Section	www.aicpa.org/interestareas/notforprofit/pages/default.aspx
Catalog of Federal Domestic Assistance (CFDA)	https://beta.sam.gov
Office of Executive Councils: Chief Financial Officers Council (CFOC)	www.cfo.gov
Department of Education: Office of Inspector General Non-Federal Audit Team	www2.ed.gov/about/offices/list/oig/nonfed/nfteam.html
Department of Health and Human Services (HHS): Office of Inspector General	www.oig.hhs.gov
Department of Housing and Urban Development (HUD): Office of Inspector General	www.hudoig.gov
Federal Audit Clearinghouse (FAC)	http://harvester.census.gov/facweb/
Federal Reserve Board	www.federalreserve.gov
FASB	www.fasb.org
Government Accountability Office (GAO)	www.gao.gov 2011 Revision of *Government Auditing Standards*: www.gao.gov/yellowbook Green Book: www.gao.gov/greenbook/overview
GASB	www.gasb.org
Government Publishing Office access	www.gpo.gov/fdsys/
Grants.gov	www.grants.gov
Council of the Inspectors General on Integrity and Efficiency (IGnet)	www.ignet.gov/

Organization	*Website*
Office of Management and Budget (OMB)	www.whitehouse.gov/omb/ OMB circulars: www.whitehouse.gov/omb/circulars/ Uniform Guidance: Title 2 CFR Part 200, *Uniform Administrative Requirements, Cost Principles, and Audit Requirements for Federal Awards*
Public Company Accounting Oversight Board (PCAOB)	www.pcaob.org
USA.gov	www.usa.gov
USAspending.gov	www.usaspending.gov

.149 The websites of the governmental practices of some of the larger CPA firms may also contain industry-specific auditing and accounting information that is helpful to auditors.